GAME-CHANGING SOCCER MOMENTS

BY NICK HUNTER

CAPSTONE PRESS
a capstone imprint

Published by Capstone Press, an imprint of Capstone
1710 Roe Crest Drive, North Mankato, Minnesota 56003
capstonepub.com

Copyright © 2025 by Capstone. All rights reserved. No part of this publication may be reproduced in whole or in part, or stored in a retrieval system, or transmitted in any form or by any means, electronic, mechanical, photocopying, recording, or otherwise, without written permission of the publisher.

SPORTS ILLUSTRATED KIDS is a trademark of ABG-SI LLC. Used with permission.

Library of Congress Cataloging-in-Publication Data is available on the Library of Congress website.
ISBN: 9781669075844 (hardcover)
ISBN: 9781669075790 (paperback)
ISBN: 9781669075806 (ebook pdf)

Summary: Game-changing moments have happened throughout soccer's history. From the star players who score match-winning goals to incredible comebacks and fan celebrations, readers will experience the excitement of unforgettable moments on the pitch.

Editor: Erika L. Shores; Designer: Sofiia Rovinskaia; Media Researcher: Jo Miller; Production Specialist: Tori Abraham

Image Credits
Alamy: Daniel Motz, 9, diebilderwelt, 5, PA Images, 8, 13; Associated Press: Carlo Fumagalli, File, 15, Dusan Vranic, 25, Francois Mori, File, 27; Getty Images: Al Messerschmidt, 17, Bob Thomas, 11, duncan1890, 7, Fantasista, 29, Popperfoto, 23; Shutterstock: FocusStocker, Cover, (top); Sports Illustrated: Bob Rosato, 21, Jerry Cooke, Cover, (bottom left), 16, Simon Bruty, Cover, (bottom right), 19, 20

Design Elements: Shutterstock: Gojindbefs, Kucher Serhii (football), Lifestyle Graphic, Navin Penrat

Any additional websites and resources referenced in this book are not maintained, authorized, or sponsored by Capstone. All product and company names are trademarks™ or registered® trademarks of their respective holders.

TABLE OF CONTENTS

Game-Changing Moments 4
The Changing Game 6
Famous Firsts 12
Game-Changing Players 16
Shocks and Surprises 22
Magic Moments 26
    Glossary 30
    Read More 31
    Internet Sites 31
    Index 32
    About the Author 32

Words in **BOLD** are in the glossary.

GAME-CHANGING MOMENTS

On December 18, 2022, the men's national teams of France and Argentina faced each other in soccer's World Cup final. At the heart of each team were two game-changing players. Argentina's Lionel Messi had been one of the most brilliant players in soccer for many years. France's Kylian Mbappé was competing to be the world's best player with his explosive speed and skill.

The match was a close contest. It ended in a 3–3 draw after **extra time**, with Argentina winning a **penalty shootout**. During the match, Messi scored twice with Mbappé claiming three goals. Game-changing players shaped a great match.

The 2022 World Cup tournament itself was game-changing. It was held for the first time in the desert country of Qatar. Air-conditioned stadiums helped players deal with extreme heat. The Qatar World Cup brought soccer to new fans.

Lionel Messi of Argentina (left) and Kylian Mbappé of France during the 2022 World Cup

THE CHANGING GAME

Game-changing moments have happened throughout soccer's history. These have made soccer the most popular sport in the world.

MAKING THE RULES

In the 1800s, lots of different games of football were played across England. In some games, players could carry the ball while in others they were only allowed to kick the ball. In 1863, several teams agreed on a set of rules that they all would follow. This group called themselves the Football Association. They named the game "association football," or "soccer" for short.

The first American college football game was played in 1869. Like soccer, rules for American football and rugby were based on the early forms of football played in England.

A match between teams from England and Scotland in 1872

GLOBAL GAME CHANGERS

Teams from England and Scotland played each other in **international** matches starting in 1872. Soccer's popularity soon spread around the world. The real game changer for international soccer was the first World Cup in 1930.

Uruguay in South America was the first **host** country of the World Cup. One-fifth of all the men in Uruguay were in the stadium as the hosts faced their neighbors Argentina in the final. Uruguay won 4–2 after falling behind. Held every four years, the World Cup is still the biggest prize in soccer.

Uruguay's men's national team won the first World Cup.

Women's soccer had to wait another 60 years for a game-changing global tournament. The first Women's World Cup was played in China in 1991. The U.S. team faced Norway in the final, winning with two goals from Michelle Akers.

The U.S. national team won the first Women's World Cup.

Today, around 30 million girls and women play organized soccer around the world.

SUPER EAGLES

Only teams from Europe and South America have won the World Cup. However, brilliant players come from all over the world. The Super Eagles of Nigeria were not expecting soccer medals at the 1996 Olympic Games. After beating mighty Brazil in the semifinal, Nigeria believed they could win. On August 3, 1996, they defeated Argentina 3–2 to win the gold medal. This was a great moment for Nigeria and African football.

GAME-CHANGING TECHNOLOGY

Since 2018, modern technology has made big changes to top-level soccer. A video assistant referee (VAR) team watches the game on screen. They support the referee with decisions such as **offside** rules and awarding penalties. Some people argue that this has spoiled the game by slowing it down.

The men's team from Nigeria won the gold medal at the 1996 Olympics in Atlanta.

FAMOUS FIRSTS

For every change in soccer, someone has to be the first to do it. Often the game is changed by the skills and ideas of players and coaches.

TOTAL FOOTBALL

In the 1970s, the Netherlands national team invented a new way of playing. They called it "total football." Team manager Rinus Michels gave his players freedom to show their skills and did not expect the team to play in fixed positions. Johan Cruyff was the most exciting player on this team. Although Cruyff's team lost in the final of the 1974 World Cup, the team's style of play inspired many others. Manager Pep Guardiola has used "total football" tactics to win trophies with Barcelona and Manchester City.

Johan Cruyff is one of the only players to have a skill named after him. He showed the world the "Cruyff turn" during the 1974 World Cup. This skillful trick enables a player to change direction with the ball and avoid a defender.

PENALTY SHOOTOUT

In 1982, teams from France and West Germany played an epic World Cup semifinal. After 30 minutes extra time, the score was 3–3. For the first time, a World Cup game was settled with a tense penalty shootout. Each team took five penalties. West Germany won to reach the final.

Since 1982, many big games have been decided by penalties. Winning and losing players feel great joy or sadness, especially the players whose penalties are saved. In 1994, the World Cup final ended in a shootout for the first time. Brazil won to claim soccer's biggest trophy.

FROM PLAYER TO PRESIDENT

In 1995, the World Player of the Year award was given to an African player for the first time. George Weah was born in Liberia but played for clubs in Europe. As a quick and skillful striker, Weah inspired many young African players. After retiring, he became president of Liberia—the first **professional** soccer player to lead his country.

George Weah with the Golden Ball trophy, given to the World Player of the Year

GAME-CHANGING PLAYERS

Great players change the game with their skill and star quality. Soccer was never the same after the careers of these game changers.

PERFECT PELÉ

Brazil is the most successful soccer nation. Brazil's winning run began in 1958 when a 17-year-old **genius** joined the team. Pelé was a great athlete, scoring goals with both feet and leaping above defenders to head the ball. Brazil's first World Cup win was in 1958, and Pelé is the only player to have won three times. His skill and personality charmed fans around the world.

AMERICAN PIONEER

Mia Hamm was another powerful goal-scorer who changed the game for others. Hamm played 276 games for the U.S. women's team. She played in the first four Women's World Cups and the first three Olympic soccer competitions, winning two of each. Hamm was also a key player in the first professional women's league. Hamm and other **pioneers** set the path for the global popularity of women's soccer.

STAR QUALITY

David Beckham's soccer skills were only one reason why he changed the game. Beckham was a midfielder for teams such as Manchester United, Real Madrid, LA Galaxy, and England. Thanks to his movie-star looks and marriage to a pop star, Beckham became famous around the world. Even people who knew little about soccer could recognize David Beckham. His fame was the start of a new **era** when soccer players could be global stars.

PERFECT FREE KICK

David Beckham scored stunning goals from free kicks. What are the secrets of the perfect free kick?

- Watch the goalkeeper and defenders to figure out where to place the ball.
- Have a controlled run-up to the ball.
- Don't try to kick the ball too hard. Concentrate on lifting it over the defenders and out of the goalkeeper's reach.
- Practice whenever you can!

MAGICAL MARTA

Brazil's women's national team has never won the World Cup, but Brazilian striker Marta is the top goal-scorer in the tournament. Marta began playing soccer on the street, outplaying everyone with her magical dribbling skills. She has been named FIFA World Player of the Year six times and works with the United Nations to give girls more chances to succeed in sports.

SUPER SKILLS

Strength and power are important to every soccer team. But Lionel Messi relies on skills that only the best players have. He can see a pass or a goal-scoring chance that others miss. Playing for Barcelona and Paris Saint-Germain, Messi has won every club trophy there is. He won the World Cup with Argentina in 2022. Messi is proof that superb skills are the secret of soccer greatness.

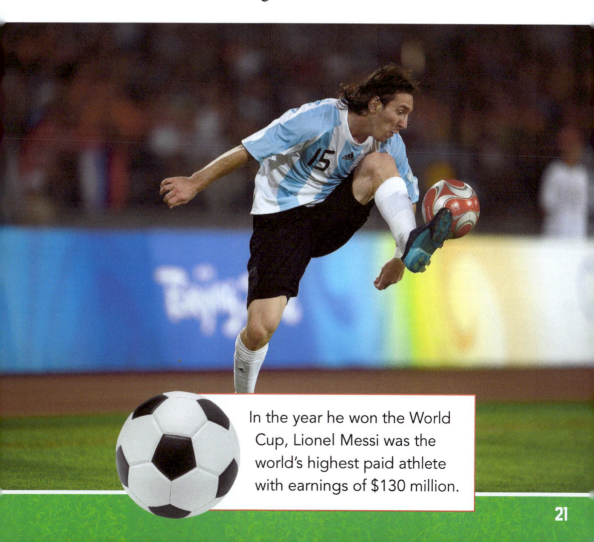

In the year he won the World Cup, Lionel Messi was the world's highest paid athlete with earnings of $130 million.

SHOCKS AND SURPRISES

In soccer, you can never be sure what will happen. A single goal can change a game, which means that even the best team can be beaten.

SHOCKING RESULTS

Only eight different countries have won the World Cup, but there is room for plenty of surprises on the way. Argentina's team were champions in 2022, but the competition started with one of the biggest World Cup shocks when they were beaten 2–1 by Saudi Arabia.

The biggest shock of all happened way back in 1950. England played against the U.S. team. No one expected the American players to challenge England's professional stars. The U.S. team's 1–0 victory shocked the world.

U.S. player Joe Gaetjens (right) scored the winning goal against England in the 1950 World Cup.

MIRACLE WINS

Any team can spring a surprise in a single game, but over a season the best team wins the league. That is often the team with the richest owners or the most fans, who can buy a squad of star players. The English Premier League includes world-famous clubs like Manchester City, Liverpool, and Arsenal. With competition like that, experts thought Leicester City had a one in 5,000 chance of winning in 2016.

Leicester coach Claudio Ranieri led a skillful and determined team. As other teams dropped points, Leicester stayed strong and kept winning. At the end of the season, they were champions.

GREAT COMEBACKS

The game is never over until the final whistle. In 2005, English club Liverpool were facing defeat in the Champions League final. AC Milan led 3–0 at halftime. Liverpool fought back with three second-half goals and eventually won the trophy in a penalty shootout. Liverpool fans called the comeback "the Miracle of Istanbul" after the city where it was played.

Liverpool goalkeeper Jerzy Dudek saves a penalty shot during the 2005 Champions League final.

MAGIC MOMENTS

Some game-changing moments are not great examples of skill, but they become part of the story of soccer.

"HAND OF GOD"

Diego Maradona was a game-changing player, with magic in his feet. He is also remembered for a moment when the ball did not touch his foot. In 1986, Argentina played England in the World Cup quarter-final game. For Argentina's first goal, Maradona jumped and beat the much-bigger goalkeeper. TV replays showed that Maradona had punched the ball into the net with his hand. The referee had not spotted it. Minutes later in the game, Maradona dribbled the ball through England's defense to score one of the greatest goals ever. He said his first goal had been scored by the "hand of God."

CELEBRATIONS

Sometimes, players plan a special goal celebration when they score. After scoring against England in the 2019 Women's World Cup, U.S. player Alex Morgan mimed sipping a cup of tea. Morgan wanted to try something different from teammate Megan Rapinoe's celebration with arms stretched out.

U.S. player Alex Morgan held her hand to her mouth as if she was sipping a cup of tea.

GREAT FAN MOMENTS

Songs and chants from fans can help national and club teams play their best. Brazil's fans are famous for the samba music they play in the stands. Ghana's fans also bring colorful clothing and music to support their team. Japan's supporters cheered their team with passion at the 2022 World Cup, but they also tidied up the stadium after the game.

In 2020, many soccer games were played in empty stadiums. This was because of restrictions due to the COVID-19 pandemic. Silent stadiums were much less exciting. This showed the game-changing importance of cheering and singing supporters.

WHAT'S YOUR FAVORITE?

Player and fan celebrations show how much soccer means to people. What's your favorite game-changing moment? It could be a great comeback by your favorite team or a brilliant goal you scored yourself.

Fans waved plastic trash bags at the 2022 World Cup match between Japan and Costa Rica.

GLOSSARY

era (ERR-uh)—a period of time, usually lasting many years

extra time (EX-truh TYME)—time added when a soccer game ends in a tie, usually in a knockout game where one side needs to win

genius (GEE-nyuhs)—a person who has great intelligence or talent for doing something

host (HOHST)—a person or organization receiving others as guests; the country where a World Cup is played is the host

international (in-tur-NASH-uh-nuhl)—including more than one country

offside (OFF-side)—a soccer rule; a player is offside if they are ahead of the last defender in the opponent's half when the ball is played to them by a teammate

penalty shootout (PEN-uhl-tee SHOOT-out)—a way of deciding a tied match when both teams take penalty kicks and the team scoring most is the winner

pioneer (pye-uh-NEER)—a leader or the first person to do something

professional (pruh-FEH-shuh-nuhl)—a person who makes money by doing an activity that other people might do without pay

READ MORE

Bader, Bonnie. *What Is the World Cup?* New York: Penguin Workshop, 2023.

DK Eyewitness: *Soccer.* New York: Penguin Random House, 2023.

Jökulsson, Illugi. *Stars of Women's Soccer.* New York: Abbeville Press, 2021.

INTERNET SITES

FIFA Official Website
fifa.com

Sports Illustrated Kids: Soccer
sikids.com/tag/soccer

United States Olympic & Paralympic Museum: Mia Hamm
usopm.org/mia-hamm/

INDEX

AC Milan, 24
Akers, Michelle, 9
Argentina, 4, 5, 8, 10, 21, 22, 26
Arsenal, 24

Barcelona, 12, 21
Beckham, David, 18
Brazil, 10, 14, 16, 28
Brazil women's national team, 20

Champions League, 24, 25
Costa Rica, 29
Cruyff, Johan, 12, 13

Dudek, Jerzy, 25

England, 6, 7, 8, 18, 22, 23, 26
English Premier League, 24

Football Association, 6
France, 4, 5, 14

Gaetjens, Joe, 23
Ghana, 28
Guardiola, Pep, 12

Hamm, Mia, 17

Japan, 28, 29

LA Galaxy, 18
Leicester City, 24
Liberia, 14
Liverpool, 24

Manchester City, 12, 24
Manchester United, 18
Maradona, Diego, 26
Marta, 20
Mbappé, Kylian, 4, 5
Messi, Lionel, 4, 5, 21
Michels, Rinus, 12
Morgan, Alex, 27

Netherlands, the, 12
Nigeria, 10, 11
Norway, 9

Olympic Games, 10, 11, 17

Paris Saint-Germain, 21
Pelé, 16

Rapinoe, Megan, 27
Real Madrid, 18

Saudi Arabia, 22
Scotland, 7, 8

Uruguay, 8
U.S. men's team, 22
U.S. women's team, 9, 17

Weah, George, 14, 15
West Germany, 14
Women's World Cup, 9, 17, 27
World Cup, 4, 5, 8, 10, 12, 13, 14, 16, 20–23, 26, 28, 29

ABOUT THE AUTHOR

Nick Hunter has written more than 100 books for young people. He specializes in writing about history, social studies, and sports. Nick lives in Oxford, UK, with his wife and two sports-loving sons. His favorite soccer teams are Norwich City and England.